Children of the World

Tanzania

For a free color catalog describing Gareth Stevens' list of high-quality children's books, call 1-800-341-3569 (USA) or 1-800-461-9120 (Canada).

For their help in the preparation of *Children of the World: Tanzania*, the editors gratefully thank Alfred Boma, Yusuf Kalala, and Raya Mohammed of the Embassy of the United Republic of Tanzania, Washington, DC, and Oswald Bwechwa, student at Marquette University, Milwaukee, Wisconsin.

Library of Congress Cataloging-in-Publication Data

Tanzania.

   (Children of the world)
   Includes index.
   Summary: Presents the life of a twelve-year-old boy living in a village at the foot of Mount Kilimanjaro in Tanzania describing his family, home, school, and amusements and some of the traditions and celebrations of his country.
   1. Tanzania—Social life and customs—Juvenile literature. 2. Children—Tanzania—Juvenile literature. [1. Family life—Tanzania. 2. Tanzania—Social life and customs] I. Nakamura, Haruko, ill. II. Weber, Valerie. III. Pelnar, Tom. IV. Series: Children of the world (Milwaukee, Wis.)
DT442.5.T35 1989   967.8'04   88-42890

ISBN 1-55532-210-7 (lib. bdg.)

North American edition first published in 1989 by

Gareth Stevens Children's Books
RiverCenter Building, Suite 201
1555 North RiverCenter Drive
Milwaukee, Wisconsin 53212, USA

This work was originally published in shortened form consisting of section I only. Photographs and original text copyright © 1988 by Haruko Nakamura. First and originally published by Kaisei-sha Publishing Co., Ltd., Tokyo. World English rights arranged with Kaisei-sha Publishing Co., Ltd. through Japan Foreign Rights Centre.

Copyright this format © 1989 by Gareth Stevens, Inc. Additional material and maps copyright © 1989 by Gareth Stevens, Inc.

Series Editor: Rhoda Irene Sherwood
Editor: Valerie Weber
Design: Kristi Ludwig
Research Editor: Scott Enk
Map Design: Sheri Gibbs

Printed in the United States of America

1 2 3 4 5 6 7 8 9 95 94 93 92 91 90

Children of the World

Tanzania

Photography
by Haruko
Nakamura

Edited by
Valerie Weber &
Tom Pelnar

Gareth Stevens Publishing
MILWAUKEE

. . . a note about *Children of the World*:

The children of the world live in fishing towns, Arctic regions, and urban centers, on islands and in mountain valleys, on sheep ranches and fruit farms. This series follows one child in each country through the pattern of his or her life. Candid photographs show the children with their families, at school, at play, and in their communities. The text describes the dreams of the children and often, through their own words, tells how they see themselves and their lives.

Each book also explores events that are unique to the country in which the child lives, including festivals, religious ceremonies, and national holidays. The *Children of the World* series does more than tell about foreign countries. It introduces the children of each country and shows readers what it is like to be a child in that country.

. . . and about *Tanzania*:

Twelve-year-old Rajabu lives with his large family in Kivo, a small farming village surrounded by corn fields in the United Republic of Tanzania. Like many other Tanzanian children, Rajabu enjoys making his own toys and playing games, but he also works hard in the fields, at home, and in school.

To enhance this book's value in libraries and classrooms, comprehensive reference sections include up-to-date information about Tanzania's geography, language, currency, education, culture, industry, and natural resources. *Tanzania* also features a bibliography, research topics, activity projects, and discussions of such subjects as tourism and wildlife, the country's political system, history, ethnic and religious composition, and language.

The living conditions and experiences of children in Tanzania vary tremendously according to economic, environmental, and ethnic circumstances. The reference sections help to bring to life for young readers the richness and complexity of the culture and heritage of Tanzania. Of particular interest are the discussions of the history, wildlife, and Tanzania's ideas about the best form of government for an emerging African nation.

CONTENTS

LIVING IN TANZANIA:
   Rajabu, in the Shadow of Kilimanjaro 6

Starting the Day 10
Going to Makaa Pumuwani School 12
Rajabu, the Student 14
Sacred Fire 18
The Children at Play 19
Harvesting Baobab Fruit 25
The Children at Work 26
Families Working Together 29
Soko, the Market 33
The Town of Moshi 35
Hair: A Way to Express Personality 36
Village Life 39
Mealtime 40
Evening Fun 45

FOR YOUR INFORMATION: Tanzania 48

Official name and Capital 48
History 48
Government 51
Language 52
Population and Ethnic Groups 52
Currency 53
Religion 54
Education 54
Arts 54
Sports and Recreation 55
Agriculture 55
Map 56
Land 58
Climate 58
Wildlife and Tourism 58
Industry and Commerce 59
Natural Resources 60
Dar-es-Salaam 60
Tanzanians in North America 60
Glossary of Useful Tanzanian Terms 61
More Books About Tanzania 61
Things to Do — Research Projects 61
More Things to Do — Activities 62
Index 63

Rajabu and some of his family. From left: his older sisters Mwamini and Fatuma; his mother, Mwajuma; his niece Zania; his father, Hassan; his younger sister Zainab; and Rajabu.

LIVING IN TANZANIA:
Rajabu, in the Shadow of Kilimanjaro

"Jambo!" (Hello!) "My name is Rajabu Juma and I'm 12 years old." Rajabu lives with his family in the village of Kiuo in Tanzania. Rajabu has nine brothers and sisters, but only four of them still live at home. The older ones have married and live in the village or work in the city.

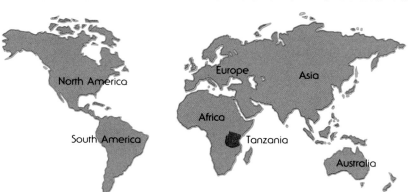

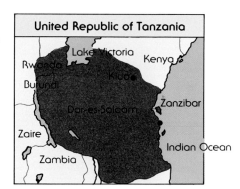

United Republic of Tanzania

Rajabu's father built these two houses from mud bricks and tree limbs. Rajabu's older sister and her family live in one of them.

Rajabu's older brother Abdullah.

Mount Kilimanjaro rises majestically above Rajabu's village of Kiuo.

Separated by trees and vegetable gardens, scattered households form a village.

The children wash the dishes from last night's supper while Rajabu takes a quick bath.

Starting the Day

No towel needed in this warm, dry air!

Rajabu awakens before sunrise to the sound of his mother milking the cows and of Fatuma, his older sister, hauling the water buckets to the village well to be filled. He runs outside to start his daily chores too, driving the family's herd of nine cows from the acacia fence to a pasture.

Then Rajabu washes himself. Because water is hard to get, he uses only two cupfuls to wash himself. The arid air will dry him as he walks to school.

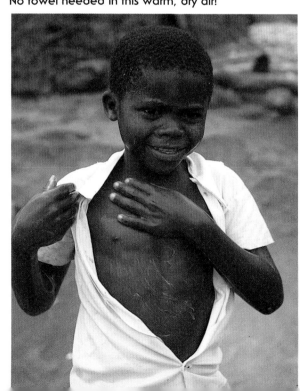

For breakfast, Rajabu sometimes has a cup of *uji*, a soupy cereal made of cornmeal mixed in hot water, but usually he eats nothing. He drops a notebook and pencil into the school bag that he made from an old *kanga*, a piece of cloth used for women's clothing. Now he's ready for school.

After saying good-by to his parents, Rajabu begins his walk to school. The school is in a village nearby and children from a number of the neighboring villages attend there.

Rajabu and his friend Rassuri.

While Rajabu and Rassuri head for school one way, other children herd their family's cattle in the opposite direction.

Rajabu's school bag, made from a worn kanga.

It takes Rajabu about 20 minutes to walk there from his small farming village surrounded by corn fields. On the way, he meets his friend Rassuri. Although Rassuri is two grades ahead of Rajabu, they are close friends. There are 15 children and lots of activity in Rassuri's family, so Rajabu loves to visit his friend's lively home.

11

Munching corn, the friends take a rocky path.

"Ready, set, run!"

Going to Makaa Pumuwani School

Rajabu and Rassuri meet with their other friends as they walk the dirt path to school. Their friend Majuma has a special treat today, a jar of corn kernels to snack on during recess. But the boys just can't wait — they eat a few as they walk along.

Rajabu tells his friends of the trouble he had herding the cows that morning. Just before he had driven them into the pasture, one cow, "the nosy one" as he calls it, discovered an empty grain container on the side of the path. Curious and smelling a possible snack, she poked her head in the bucket. There it stuck while the cow shook her head in vain, trying to free herself.

Before Rajabu can reveal how he rescued the cow, Rassuri yells, "We're late!" and Rajabu and his friends start a friendly race to school. Shoes just seem to get in Rajabu's way, so he takes them off to run faster.

Morning assembly.

With the ringing of the bell, school begins.

At least Rajabu is paying attention to the task!

Before classes begin, Rajabu and the other students clean the school building. They also sweep the courtyard with branches they have taken from trees. Then all the students gather for morning assembly before scattering to their classrooms.

There are almost 400 students in the Makaa Pumuwani Elementary School. Every grade level from one through seven has one class each, except for 2nd grade, which has two. Because there aren't enough classrooms, the 2nd grade must be divided into two sessions, morning and afternoon.

Rajabu, the Student

After morning assembly, Rajabu goes to his class and sits at his desk. When Madam Ruty enters the room, all the students stand. The children greet her politely, saying *"Shikamoo"* — a Swahili greeting that implies respect for one's elders.

Most children start school at the age of seven, but some parents keep children home longer to work in the house and fields and to help care for younger brothers and sisters. So each grade has children of different ages studying at the same level. In fact, Rajabu did not start school until he was ten years old, partially because he had to take care of his father's cattle and help with the farming, and partially because he was smaller than his other classmates. So he attends the morning session of 2nd grade.

There are supposed to be 23 children in Rajabu's class, but only 18 are attending this morning. The other children are working in the fields and doing chores for their families. It's rare for all the children to be there at once.

Morning classes are from 8:00 a.m. to 11:10 a.m. The periods are each 30 minutes long and there is one ten-minute break.

During first and second periods today, Rajabu's class studies Swahili, the national language of Tanzania. Swahili is based on Bantu, one of the major African languages. Swahili also has many words from other languages brought by non-African settlers such as Arabic, English, Hindi, and Portuguese. The second official language is English because the British used to govern this country and promoted its use in the schools. But when most people meet with their friends, they speak in one of many tribal languages, including some dialects with "click" sounds.

The principal teaches English to the older children.

Rajabu's 2nd-grade class waves "Hello" to children from other lands.

The school keeps the textbooks for the students' use year after year. Rajabu's job is to take the textbooks from a shelf in the principal's office and hand them to his classmates. Next to physical education, Swahili is Rajabu's favorite subject, and he listens carefully to Madam Ruty. At the end of the lesson, she gives a quiz to see if everyone has understood. Rajabu's grade was second in the class, so he's pleased with himself.

During third period, the children study arithmetic. Today fractions are the topic. Knowing math is useful, Rajabu realizes, but it's a difficult subject for him. Today, though, he gets a fraction problem correct and all the students clap for him. This makes Rajabu feel proud. "The best student in the class is Joseph, then comes Hamisa, and I'm third — but I'm best in soccer," declares Rajabu.

Swahili class. The students respect their teacher and listen quietly and carefully to the lesson.

The children are eager to learn all that they can. Schools in Tanzania encourage children to learn subjects that will help them become useful members of their villages. Over 80% of all Tanzanians have now learned to read and write.

The teacher checks the students' work.

Everyone seems to know the answer to this question!

"I got it!" . . . "No, it's mine!"

Rajabu's arithmetic notebook.

An arithmetic textbook and Swahili notebook.

Fourth period is Rajabu's favorite class — physical education. The students usually have to wad up paper to make a ball, but today they are lucky. The principal has borrowed a real ball from a nearby school to teach them how to play volleyball. But they are used to soccer, so they use their head and feet when the ball flies their way. Since in volleyball, the ball can only be hit with the hands, this first game goes poorly.

Now classes for today are over. Tomorrow, a sacred ceremonial fire, the Torch, will pass the school.

Finally, the Uhuru Torch arrives!

Houses decorated for the big event.

Surrounded by hibiscus and bougainvillea blossoms.

After the torch moves on, the dancing continues.

Sacred Fire

Once a year, in celebration of Tanzania's day of independence in 1961, the *Uhuru*, or Freedom, Torch is carried to every town and village. This ceremony gives people a feeling of freedom, courage, and hope.

When the torch appears in front of the crowd of teachers and students, a huge cheer fills the air. The older children, who have bells attached to their ankles, begin a dance of welcome. Flowers and dust fill the air.

Whenever friends get together, it's time for soccer.

The Children at Play

After school, the children find time for games in between their chores. The boys' favorite game is soccer. They use a homemade ball made of newspaper or plastic wadded up and tied with string. Sometimes Rajabu gets so involved he forgets to bring the cows home at dusk and must run to the pasture after dark to herd them into their corral.

Their homemade ball.

The boys practice soccer barefoot.

19

There are only a few toys for sale in the nearby town. They are mostly from other countries and are usually more costly than most people can afford. So the children collect materials from the objects around them and make their own toys, spending hours absorbed in their task.

Few people own cars or trucks in Tanzania. Many children, including Rajabu, dream of becoming a driver one day. Sometimes, when a bus or truck drives through the village, the children run after it with whoops and cries. But when following a vehicle is not satisfying enough, the children try to build their own ideal car, truck, or bus.

Rajabu concentrates on his whittling.

He uses anything around him as a tool.

Rajabu is quite proud of his collection of trucks and cars.

Rajabu is pleased with the toy truck he built, carving with a *panga*, a kind of machete, and hammering with a rock. He explains, "The body is an oil can. I made the tires from old rubber thongs and wood, and I made the steering wheel from branches. I use thorns from the acacia tree for nails. These little pebbles are the passengers and baggage. It's finished for now, but I'll keep improving my truck as I think of better parts."

This steering wheel looks almost like a real one.

It's like driving your own car.

"Keep your foot off the hopscotch line!"

Playhouses made of sugar-cane husks.

Corn husks provide a tumbling ground.

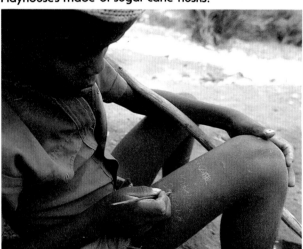

Rajabu uses his thigh as a notepad.

A game called *bento*, like marbles.

Many girls form dolls from clay and rags or instruments from empty cans and rubber bands. Other favorite games include dodge ball and hopscotch.

Sometimes Rajabu plays hopscotch with his younger sister and their friends. When they get near the end of the markings, they must close their eyes and try not to step on the lines. Sometimes Rajabu's younger sister peeks — a good way to start a quarrel.

Rajabu flies a kite he made at school. Schoolchildren have one *sanaa* (crafts) class each week.

A toy bicycle.

Rag dolls.

A slingshot.

Mud dolls and a doll house.

23

Rajabu climbs the towering baobab.

Harvesting Baobab Fruit

After school, Rajabu and his friends sometimes hike to the mountains to pick baobab fruit, a favorite snack. They throw rocks to make the fruit fall. If that doesn't work, the boys climb the huge trees, which can grow up to 60 feet (18 m) high and 30 feet (9 m) around.

Ripe fruit will fall by itself, but the boys can't wait.

The baobab fruit is shaped like a football.

Rajabu grins, looking forward to his favorite snack.

Tasty white pulp surrounds the seeds.

Baobab pulp mixed with water tastes like soda pop!

Rajabu's father and his niece Sarima store the harvested corn.

The Children at Work

Rajabu and his friends watch their parents and older brothers and sisters in their work and imitate what they do. In this way, they start to take on new and helpful roles in their families.

In Tanzania, most children must work almost as hard as the adults. Rajabu mends his own clothes, takes care of the cows and goats, and helps to harvest the crops.

While the country has many different kinds of soils and much of the land is moderately fertile, only about 10% of the land is cultivated. The government owns the land, and people can grow crops on any land that is not being used by other farmers.

While their parents work in the field, the children take the corn kernels off the cobs.

Because there are few places to store excess crops and few large markets to sell them to, most Tanzanians grow only as much food as they can use. This is called subsistence farming. Subsistence farmers grow mainly corn, millet, rice, sorghum, cassava, bananas, coconuts, and pulses. Like Rajabu's family, they may sell any excess crops in small local markets or trade them for the goods they need. As cash crops for export, other farmers grow tea, coffee, tobacco, spices, nuts, cloves, cotton, and sisal, which is a fiber that is made into rope.

"Watch out for that splashing!"

Two friends move the wheelbarrow.

Rajabu's friends also help with the family's work. They know that if they work together, it will not only be more fun, but they will also have more time to play!

In addition, doing work together lightens everyone's load. Washing everyone's clothes in one basin instead of several means that they have to carry home less water from the village well.

Rajabu and his cousins sing on the way to the bean field.

Families Working Together

The whole family, including cousins, gathers together to do the large farming chores, such as picking *maharagwe*, a kind of bean. Because it is a two-hour walk each way to the field, they must start early, around 5:00 a.m.

The children gather the pods in one place.

The group's pace quickens as they head for home.

Playing in the water brings relief from the heat.

Before leaving for the bean field, Rajabu and his cousins have some uji. They chat as they walk along the dusty country lanes. Rajabu plans on doing his laundry in the river near the maharagwe field, so he carries his dirty clothes on his head.

The sun beats down on them as they reach the field. Each of Rajabu's older sisters shields her head from the sun with a kanga, the ankle-length cloth that women usually wear wrapped around their waist.

The group stops for a drink of water and then begins to pick the beans. The dried pods are scattered on the ground, mixed with weeds. They haul all the piles of pods to one place.

To make the work seem easier, someone starts to sing and they all join in. Rajabu's older sisters love to sing and dance. Whether they are doing the wash, working in the fields, or doing other household chores, the singing and movement can make even hot, monotonous labor seem to go faster.

During the hottest part of the day, Rajabu and his cousins slip away to the river to do their laundry. Washing clothes at home is hard because they have to use the village well water sparingly. So Rajabu likes to wash in the river, where he can use all the water he wants. When the laundry is clean, it's time to splash! The children take off their clothes and jump in the river. After the hot, dusty work, the water feels great!

30

On the way, they pass a corn field after harvest.

Rajabu's mother tosses the beans, letting the chaff fall.

When the children get back to the field, they heap mounds of bean pods onto straw mats to carry them home. There, they will spread the pods in the yard to dry and then beat them between two sticks to separate the beans from the pods. Finally, Rajabu's mother will shake the beans in a bamboo basket to sift out the chaff, the remaining bits of pods and weeds.

As the sun begins to set, Rajabu and his family start for home, carrying the bean pods in bags on their heads. Their steps are not as light as they were when coming to the field, and their songs are quieter. After a hard day's work, they are eager for their evening meal.

31

The Kibororooni market. The bargaining is fierce but friendly.

Fatuma inspects a shirt.

Hollow gourds hold milk.

Piles of potatoes await purchase.

Friends and family wait for the bus.

Trucks carry their purchases back to the village.

Soko, the Market

Today is Saturday, one of Rajabu's favorite days because it's market day in the nearby town of Kiborooroni, an exciting and lively place. He helps his family bring their corn and milk to the market to sell. Then he tours the market, looking at all the food, secondhand clothing, and household items for sale.

After they sell all their goods, Rajabu's family uses the money to buy soap, oil, vegetables, and other things for their household. Rajabu even gets a new shirt, but he will have to share it with his sister.

33

The town of Moshi is famous as a base for people climbing Mount Kilimanjaro.

Moshi's only movie theater. A jewelry vendor's stall.

Medicine bottles in a pharmacy.

Fruit, vegetables, and baskets.

A bookstore with Tanzanian crafts.

A general store.

An ice cream would be a real treat!

Imported goods.

A roadside market.

Watching the cobblers at work.

Thongs made from old tires.

The Town of Moshi

This is a big day for Rajabu! His parents have allowed him to go with his older brother Abdullah by bus to Moshi, a town he has only visited once before. Hoping to buy himself a treat, he carefully puts his entire savings of 40 shillings, worth about 28 cents, into his shirt pocket. There are so many wonderful things to look at and possibly to buy in town. "When we go, let's get some *mandazi* (fried bread) to take home!" he shouts excitedly.

A useful hairstyle for a student.

Of course, not everyone has enough hair for a lot of braids.

Hair: A Way to Express Personality

All over Tanzania, and indeed much of Africa, you can see a wide variety of hairstyles on the women and girls. It's one way they adorn themselves. At twilight after they have finished work or while waiting in line at the village well, the women and girls braid each other's hair whenever and wherever it's convenient.

If the style is simple and the hair short, braiding only takes about 30 minutes. But braiding long hair into a complicated style can take more than two hours. All this time together has benefits, though — the women and girls can use it to discuss the things that concern them.

There are dozens of ways to style hair creatively.

36

This style is called the Statue of Liberty.

A mother braiding.

A variety of ways to wear hair.

Fatuma carries water.

What a face!

Brushing his teeth with a twig.

He uses a razor to cut his nails.

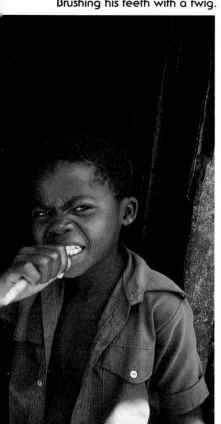

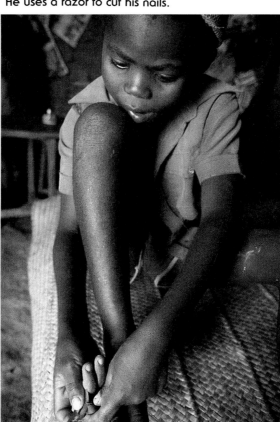

There are always many people lining up to get water at the village well. People chat or do small tasks while they wait.

Village Life

With only a tiny stream trickling from the one well in the village, people must wait in line for a long time to fill their buckets. Rajabu tries this job, but he can't carry the heavy bucket as well as his sisters can.

Rajabu works hard at his tasks. He tries to do things for himself — cleaning his room once a week and mending his torn clothing. He also tears pages from used notebooks and folds them into wallets.

Small children often help with cooking.

Fatuma uses corncobs to build a hot fire.

Preparing a squash dish.

Mealtime

Because Rajabu works and plays hard, he can hardly wait for mealtimes. The staple food in this part of Tanzania is called *ugali*. To make ugali, ground cornmeal is slowly mixed into a basin of hot water and then kneaded. Making ugali is the job of Rajabu's older sisters. Since the paste hardens gradually, the work requires strong arms and hands.

Fatuma is making soup. First she fries green vegetables and onions in a pan. Then she adds water and sometimes tomatoes or fish. The children break off some ugali and form a pocket in it with their fingers. Then they scoop some soup in and wolf down the whole thing.

"This ugali is getting too hard to turn!"

A special dish for guests.

The various tribes in Tanzania make many different kinds of food. For example, Rajabu's Pare tribe makes *pure*, a dish consisting of mixed beans, corn, and milk.

The Pare tribe has a number of cows. But like most other Tanzanian tribes except the Masai, they use their cattle only for their milk. The Masai drink not only a cow's milk but, occasionally, also its blood.

Cows are a major form of wealth in Tanzania — the more cows your family has, the richer you are. Many tribes also think of cows as a sign of prestige or use them as a dowry. The dowry is the money or property brought by a bride to her husband when they get married. All of the tribes in Tanzania use a system of dowry, but they demand different things as a dowry price — money, jewelry, clothing, food, goats, cows, or other useful items. Depending on the tribe, different relatives get part or all of the dowry.

The pure is ready to eat.

A water bucket and gourds of milk.

"No, you can't have my supper!
You already ate yours."

Children in Tanzania do not always come home to eat. If they are playing at a friend's home, their friend's family usually invites them to eat there. Rajabu often has his meals at his friend Rassuri's house.

Rajabu loves being an older brother. He likes to tell the younger children stories of his initiation. Many tribes in Tanzania have a period of training when the children are between the ages of nine and twelve. During this initiation, the boys and girls are separated and attend special classes, often leaving their families and going into the bush land. There, a village elder will teach them more about their tribe and culture and prepare them for their adult roles.

Rajabu also likes to boss the younger children around. They look up to him and admire his school uniform. Many of the children in Tanzania dress in native clothing with its brilliant colors and beautiful designs, but Western styles, like Rajabu's school uniform, are gradually becoming more common.

The children often have to share clothes and must carefully tend them. Rajabu's uniform will probably be worn by the next child going to school in his family.

As the children eat, they argue about the fable that their grandmother told them last night and try to figure out the moral. Many traditions, ideas, and codes of behavior in Tanzania are passed on through tales told by grandparents and parents.

They also talk of the things they would like to do when they are older. Of course, Rajabu would like to drive a real truck, better than the toy one he has made, or be a farmer or a ranger in a wildlife preserve.

His older brother talks of working in the diamond mines in another part of the country. The salary for miners is better than the income he could earn in their village, but he would miss his family. Tanzanian families remain close, even if members move into the city or far away. Fatuma, Rajabu's older sister, has heard tales of the sea and dreams of moving to Tanzania's seacoast, always within the sound of the water that is so rare in their village.

Today the children eat dinner before the adults do.

Rajabu and his friends dance on the beaten earth path in front of his house.

Rajabu plays with the younger children. But sometimes he overlooks a dangerous game.

His older sister teaches multiplication to Rajabu by lamplight. Few village houses have electricity.

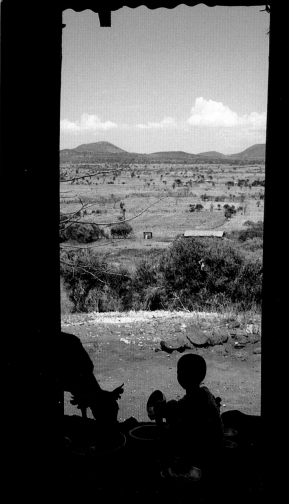

The children usually sleep in a bed, but when they have overnight guests, they spread out a cowhide to share.

The view from Rajabu's house.

Evening Fun

After supper, Rajabu works on his homework and then plays with the other children and some friends who have come for a visit.

Boom-ba-ba-boom-ba-ba-boom. . . . The sound of drums shakes Rajabu's home. The children leap up and dash outside. Once a week, the children gather without the adults to sing and dance in the moonlight. They move rhythmically to the drums, and their singing voices echo from the foot of Mount Kilimanjaro, towering black in the warm evening sky.

A herd of gnu in Ngorongoro National Park.

The main street in Dar-es-Salaam, a blend of the modern and traditional.

FOR YOUR INFORMATION: Tanzania

Official name: Jamhuri ya Muungano wa Tanzania
(jahm-HOOR-ee yah MOON-gah-noh
wah tahn-zah-KNEE-uh)
United Republic of Tanzania

Capital: Dar-es-Salaam

History

Tanzania is made up of two older countries — the mainland nation of Tanganyika and the island nation of Zanzibar, which consists of the islands of Zanzibar and Pemba. The islands and mainland have somewhat similar histories.

Early Tanzanians

People have been living in Tanzania since the dawn of the human race. Anthropologists discovered remains of humanlike beings who lived there 3.7 million years ago. By about 400 BC, their descendants, called the San people, roamed the plains in search of animals to hunt and plants to eat. Around the first century BC, farmers from the Nile Valley and the Congo Basin traveled south into the savannahs and pushed the San from the land in order to cultivate it.

At about the same time, peoples using the Bantu language also migrated into mainland Tanzania, and Bantu became the chief language group. The Bantu tribes brought knowledge of iron working and pottery making to the area. Like the settlers from the Nile and Congo, they also farmed, and either absorbed the San into their communities or forced them to retreat into less fertile areas. As each group settled, customs and languages became distinct; people began to see themselves as members of different tribes. The Bantu developed a number of kingdoms with systems of government and fairly stable economies based on farming.

Arab Invasion and the Slave Trade

About the 10th century AD, invaders from outside Africa began making forays into the area. Sailing with the monsoon winds down the eastern edge of the African coast, the Arabs found the island of Zanzibar a perfect location for trade. They wanted ivory and gold from the interior. So the Arabs traded with the local tribes, selling them glass, wheat, wine, and iron goods. Sometimes they sent out their own expeditions to search for the elephants and their ivory tusks.

This was the beginning of the slave trade in Tanzania and neighboring countries. The Arabs captured local people, forced them to carry the ivory hundreds of miles back to the coast, and then sold them to slave traders or to plantation owners. They encouraged warlike tribes to prey upon weaker tribes and to take hostages to be sold as slaves. At the height of the slave trade in the 18th century, as many as 20,000 slaves passed through the Zanzibar slave market each year. And these were a small proportion of the people captured each year to be sold — the others died on their long march from the interior.

European Conquest

During the mid-1400s, Portuguese explorers also sailed down the coast, seeking a sea route to the Indies. By 1509, they ruled the coastal areas and the islands. But they made little attempt to develop any colonies. Instead, they used the region mainly as a port for resupplying their ships and, to a lesser extent, for slaving. By the mid-1500s, they discovered a better ocean route and reduced their army in Tanzania. So by 1740, the Arabs found it relatively easy to take control again.

In contrast to the Portuguese, the Germans, who arrived later, wanted the mainland for farming and, to a lesser extent, for trade. In 1885, Germany declared the area a protectorate. The Tanzanians rebelled violently against German rule, especially from 1905 through 1907 during the Maji Maji uprisings. Over 120,000 Africans lost their lives fighting the Germans. Today, many Tanzanians consider this rebellion as the beginning of nationalism, the movement toward freeing themselves from foreign rulers.

By the late 1800s, the British had stopped their trade in slaves and began to fight to abolish other nations' slave trade in Zanzibar and Tanganyika. In 1890, Zanzibar became a British protectorate. When Germany lost World War I, the League of Nations gave control of Tanganyika to the British as part of the peace plan. The British were to train the Tanganyikans to govern their own country. Unlike previous colonizers, the British tried to rule the people through their own tribal organizations and had more respect for native law and custom. They trained the Tanganyikans in finance and administration, and the Tanganyikans gradually gained more power.

Independence and Julius Nyerere, *Mwalimu* — the Teacher

The nationalist movement in Tanganyika began in 1954 when schoolteacher Julius Nyerere and other people began the Tanganyika African National Union (TANU) in order to create an independent African nation. In 1958, they won the first national elections in Tanganyika.

Three years later, in 1961, the United Nations granted Tanganyika its independence. Julius Nyerere became Tanganyika's first president in 1962. In 1963, Zanzibar also attained independence. The two countries merged in 1964, calling their new nation Tanzania. Nyerere remained president after this merger.

Tanzania's transition from colony to independent nation was relatively peaceful compared to other African independence movements. There are at least four reasons for this. First, the British recognized that the country would become self-ruling eventually and were prepared to relinquish control. So Tanganyikans did not have to revolt to overthrow a colonial government as Africans did in other countries. Second, Tanzania had a large number of tribes; no single tribe was large enough to dominate the government. Third, unlike other African nations where many European colonists had settled for generations, Tanzania had a primarily African population, so racial strife did not undermine Nyerere's attempts to develop the country. Finally, Nyerere's moderate political attitudes and his belief that Africans must rule Africa made him popular with his people. When he retired in 1985, Ali Hassan Mwinyi became president, and Nyerere now retains the role of elder statesman and head of Tanzania's only political party.

Nyerere used three words as his guide for the new nation: *uhuru* (freedom), *umoja* (unity), and *ujamaa* (familyhood). Umoja is the principle that everyone in a group has a right to share in decision making. Ujamaa is the idea that Tanzanians should act as a family does, making decisions that improve everyone's life, not just an individual's. Nyerere believed that after so many centuries of foreign rule, these three principles would keep Tanzania free.

Tanzania Today

All this has worked rather well politically, if not economically. Tanzania is politically stable. But it is also poor, as a result of a number of factors. One is that about 80% of all Tanzanians live in the countryside. With few large cities, there is little industry and commerce. Another is that, although Tanzania has an adequate supply of natural resources such as coal and iron ore, it lacks the money to develop them. Also, it has little to export, so it cannot bring cash into the country through trade. And, finally, Tanzania has had to borrow money from other countries and remains in debt to them.

On the other hand, the country's government, based on Nyerere's ideals and blended with socialism, has modified its position on such things as government control of most industries. The government is encouraging individuals and businesses to produce more goods for the people. It is also trying to control rising prices and has reduced borrowing from other countries.

Under Nyerere's guidance and philosophy, Tanzania has also been a leader in Africa. It has supported independence and majority rule throughout Africa, providing shelter and support to independence movements in Angola, Zimbabwe, Namibia, Mozambique, and South Africa. Tanzanian forces also drove Uganda's brutal dictator, Idi Amin Dada, from power and ended his policy of widespread corruption, pillage, and murder.

Government

Tanzania has a socialist government, meaning that the government owns and controls industries. These include banks, railroads, public utilities like the phone, gas, and electric companies, the major factories, and more. In an attempt to improve the economy, it has more recently allowed individuals to own businesses and industries.

Tanzania's constitution gives great power to the president, the parliament, and the president's political party. In fact, only one party is allowed in Tanzania, the Chama Cha Mapinduzi (Revolutionary Party of Tanzania). This party's policies are usually the government's policies.

The president is elected to a five-year term. Two vice-presidents aid and advise the president. To insure fair representation, if the president is from the mainland, a vice-president must be from the islands, and vice versa. The president chooses cabinet members from the parliament, called the National Assembly.

The National Assembly, the legislative branch of government, consists of 165 representatives. Most are elected, but a few are appointed from Tanzania's 25 regions, the trade unions, and the two universities. The Chama Cha Mapinduzi must approve all candidates. The people in each district usually nominate two National Assembly members. All people over the age of 18 can vote.

The government of the United Republic directs matters affecting the entire country, including the islands. But Zanzibar and Pemba also have their own legislative and executive branches, with a 40-member Council of Representatives and a president. There are also regional, state, and village governments.

The tribes still wield some influence but they rarely affect decisions outside the tribe itself. National politicians have to appeal to everyone in the country, not just to a few powerful special interest groups or tribes.

Language

The official languages of Tanzania are Swahili and English. Swahili is derived from Bantu and is influenced by Arabic, English, Hindi, and Portuguese. But in everyday life, nearly all Tanzanians speak one of the many Bantu dialects.

Since Tanzania has so many tribes, there are also other languages. Two tribes, the Sandawe of central Tanzania and the Hadza of the north, speak a "click" language in which words are mixed with clicking sounds. It is virtually impossible for a non-native to learn this fascinating language. Wherever the Arab population is high, people speak Arabic. The Asian people in Tanzania speak several languages, but mainly those of India. Since so much of the world's work in industry, science, and technology is conducted in English, schools often teach this language.

Population and Ethnic Groups

Almost 99% of Tanzania's 22 million people are native Africans. They are referred to as Bantu people after the approximately 100 related languages they speak. The largest single group is the Sukuma, making up approximately one-eighth of the population. Other major groups are the Hehe, Zaramo, Chagga, Gogo, Nyakyusa, Yao, and Masai. About 70,000 Arabs, 54,000 Asians, and 10,000 Europeans make up most of the remaining 1%.

Most Tanzanians live in rural areas and until recently, they lived in the ancient ways. They survived mainly by subsistence farming or by herding animals. A few tribes still lived by hunting animals and gathering plants to eat. Each tribe possessed its own territory but shared languages and religions with its neighbors.

Social structures varied from tribe to tribe. Chiefs governed some tribes while the tribal elders led others. For example, the Sukuma tribe of Lake Victoria had many chiefs. But the Hehe tribe of the southern highlands had only a single chief. The Masai had neither chief nor village. They chose, instead, to make everyone free of all control.

Housing also varied depending on the tribe and the location. Traditional houses were often round or conical and made of mud and grasses or of dried cow manure. In northern Tanzania, Sukuma villages held cattle pens, grain storage sheds, and homes for a husband and his wives. Rather than living in a fixed location, the Masai followed the migrations of their cattle. They pulled up thorny bushes to make a hedge that protected themselves and their livestock from dangerous animals. Along the coast, simple villages had irregular dirt streets and pole houses.

But the old ways of life are changing. Some people are moving to the cities to find work in factories and businesses. The government has established many Ujamaa (familyhood) villages based on the idea of cooperative farming. Tribes and their chiefs now have little of the power they once had. Square buildings made of wood and stone are replacing traditional African houses.

Currency

The monetary unit of Tanzania is the shilling. One hundred *senti* make up one shilling. Coins are minted in denominations of 5, 10, 20, and 50 senti, and also 1, 5, 10, and 20 shillings. Paper money is printed in notes of 5, 10, 20, 50, 100, and 200 shillings. Like many currencies, the value of Tanzanian money changes. In 1984, one US dollar was worth 12.25 shillings. But by 1989, one US dollar was worth about 143 shillings. In other words, right now the dollar is worth more than it was. This should help the US tourist find travel in Tanzania less expensive and, in turn, help Tanzania's tourism industry. But it also means that prices are high for Tanzanians. Many cannot afford the products manufactured in their own country.

Religion

Like other traditional customs, the old systems of belief have changed in Tanzania. In the past, most Tanzanians believed in a form of religion called animism. Animists believe that animals, trees, rivers, and rocks have souls and should be respected and worshipped. They also revere their ancestors, the land, and ritual objects.

About 30% of Tanzanians are still animists and another 30% of the Tanzanians are Christian. Of these, about two-thirds are Roman Catholic. About 30% of the people are Muslim. Some Tanzanians of Asian descent are Hindu, Buddhist, or Jainist, a sect that requires strict adherence to nonviolence and forbids killing any animal.

Education

While children in Tanzania can start primary school at age five, most start at age seven. Almost 90% of all children now attend school — twice the number of students attending at independence. Because 80% of the population lives in the country, schools teach ways to farm efficiently with simple tools. Courses such as animal care and home economics also prepare children for a rural life. To encourage a sense of responsibility and group cooperation, students take care of the school buildings and grounds and help to run the school. Because the government can no longer afford to pay for all schooling, families must now pay school fees, in addition to taxes, for primary and secondary schooling.

Secondary schooling is difficult to obtain, as there are few places and students must pass an exam to enter. Although the number of secondary schools has increased, by the early 1980s, secondary schools had places for only 10% of primary school graduates. The main emphasis in secondary schools and vocational programs is on agriculture, commerce, home economics, and technical and scientific subjects.

Entrance to a university is harder to obtain. Students must work in the government, an industry, or village for two years, receive references from their co-workers and employers, show high academic achievement, and prove their devotion to national policies. They must also sign a contract promising they will serve the government for at least five years when they graduate. About 950 students graduate each year from the University of Dar-es-Salaam and the University of Agriculture at Morogoro. A new university is being built at Mbeya in southwestern Tanzania.

Arts

Traditional arts flourish in Tanzania. Each tribe has its own folklore, dances, poetry, songs, musical instruments, and wood carvings. The Zaramo make carvings of animals and people, and the Masai produce elaborate masks, shields, and spears. The Makonde carve striking abstract sculptures from ebony wood.

The Arabs of Zanzibar and the coast are famous for their intricately carved furniture and for their architecture. The Arabic buildings on Zanzibar are several stories high, whitewashed, and decorated with elaborately carved, brass-studded doors. Though neglected during the years of rule by other nations, Swahili poetry and prose now thrive. Writers are translating Swahili poetry and other kinds of literature into English. Former president Nyerere has translated Shakespeare's plays into Swahili.

Sports and Recreation

Both children and adults are soccer enthusiasts and play this game with great gusto. If they do not have a plastic or rubber ball, people wrap banana or other plant leaves until they form a solid spherical shape.

Many Tanzanian children love competitive games. They wrestle to show who is biggest and toughest or run races to test for the swiftest runner. Another popular village game is *kuyu*. With a whip made from a banana leaf, the children hit a six-inch (15 cm) wooden object shaped like a top and try to make it spin. In some tribes, the children roll a bicycle tire with a long stick to see who can make it whirl all around the village. In schools, basketball and gymnastics are gaining popularity.

In the cities, people also play sports such as squash, tennis, swimming, volleyball, and basketball. They also go to movies, sports competitions, and dance and musical performances. Kung fu movies are very popular.

Agriculture

Agriculture is the heart of Tanzania's economy. About 85% of the people work in farm-related jobs. The principal crops grown for export are coffee, tea, cotton, cashew nuts, cloves, sugar, sisal (a fiber used for rope), and certain kinds of chrysanthemums that provide pyrethrum, a chemical for insecticides. Farmers also grow peanuts, grapes for wine, and a few fruits for export. Pemba and Zanzibar are the world's leading producers of cloves. Zanzibar also exports coconuts.

Farmers grow corn, millet, rice, sorghum, potatoes, dry beans, bananas, and melons to feed their families. They also raise cattle, goats, sheep, and chickens.

The government has encouraged farmers to grow crops for sale and export, but over the past ten years, there have been problems. Recent years of drought, poor prices, decreasing demand for crops, and difficulty in getting crops to distribution centers to sell have all combined to make farmers decrease or stop growing export crops. Many farmers have returned to subsistence farming. With any excess crops they grow, they barter, often on the black market, for the goods they need.

TANZANIA — Political and Physical

GENERAL REFERENCE

Countries

TANZANIA

Towns over 100,000
- ● Mombasa

Towns under 100,000
- ○ Pangani

▬ ▪ ▬ International Boundaries

▬▬ Major Transportation Routes

━━ Rivers

SOMALIA

ETHIOPIA

SUDAN

UGANDA

KENYA

TANZANIA

RWANDA

BURUNDI

ZAIRE

Dif

Mega ○

Mombasa ●

Pemba Is.

Zanzibar Is.

Dar es Salaam

Pangani ○

Tanga ●

Bagamoyo ○

Kilosa ○

Equator

Dawa

Tana

Galana

Pangani

Wami

L. Turkana
(L. Rudolf)

Turbwe

Mt. Kenya
17,058 ft/5,199 m ▲

Nairobi ●

Nakuru ○

Kilimanjaro
19,340 ft/5,895 m ▲

Kiuo ○

Arusha ●

Meru 14,979 ft/4,566 m ▲

L. Manyara

L. Natron

L. Eyasi

Wembere

Singida ○

Dodoma ○

Rungwa

Kinyeti
10,456 ft/3,187 m ▲

Kitgum ○

Elgon
14,178 ft/4,321 m ▲

Kampala ●

Entebbe ○

Lake
Victoria

Musoma ○

Mwanza ●

Geita ○

Shinyanga ○

Tabora ○

Ugalla

L.
Mobutu
Sese Seko
(L. Albert)

L. George

L. Edward

L. Kivu

Ruwenzori
Rg.

Margherita
16,795 ft/5,119 m ▲

Butembo ○

Bukoba ○

Kigali ●

Bujumbura ●

Kigoma-Ujiji ○

Lake Tanganyika

Kalemi ○

Bakavu ●

Aruwimi

Lindi

Lowa

Ruzizi

Luama

Luvua

Lukuga

Luvu

Equator